Nebraska

THE CORNHUSKER STATE

www.av2books.com

AV² provides enriched content that supplements and complements this book. Weigl's AV² books strive to create inspired learning and engage young minds in a total learning experience.

Your AV² Media Enhanced books come alive with...

Audio
Listen to sections of the book read aloud.

Key Words
Study vocabulary, and complete a matching word activity.

Video
Watch informative video clips.

Quizzes
Test your knowledge.

Go to **www.av2books.com**, and enter this book's unique code.

BOOK CODE

N 5 1 7 3 4 6

Embedded Weblinks
Gain additional information for research.

Slide Show
View images and captions, and prepare a presentation.

AV² by Weigl brings you media enhanced books that support active learning.

Try This!
Complete activities and hands-on experiments.

... and much, much more!

Published by AV² by Weigl
350 5th Avenue, 59th Floor
New York, NY 10118
Website: www.av2books.com   www.weigl.com

Library of Congress Cataloging-in-Publication Data

Foran, Jill.
  Nebraska / Jill Foran.
     p. cm. -- (A guide to American states)
  Includes index.
  ISBN 978-1-61690-799-0 (hardcover : alk. paper) -- ISBN 978-1-61690-475-3 (online)
  1. Nebraska--Juvenile literature. I. Title.
  F666.3.F675 2011
  978.2--dc23
                        2011018339

Printed in the United States of America in North Mankato, Minnesota

052011
WEP180511

Project Coordinator Jordan McGill
Art Director Terry Paulhus

Photo Credits
Every reasonable effort has been made to trace ownership and to obtain permission to reprint copyright material. The publishers would be pleased to have any errors or omissions brought to their attention so that they may be corrected in subsequent printings.

Weigl acknowledges Getty Images as its primary image supplier for this title.

Contents

More than 9 million acres of Nebraska's land is planted in corn. About 1.5 million acres are planted in wheat.

Introduction

Nebraska is a state of treeless prairies, fertile croplands, and grassy, rolling plains. It lies halfway between the Atlantic and Pacific oceans. The Platte River flows across the state, offering its waters for **irrigation**, recreation, and the production of **hydroelectric** power. The Platte's broad valley is an important transportation **corridor**, linking eastern and western Nebraska. It has provided a path for thousands of travelers throughout history. The river is also indirectly responsible for the state's name. The Oto, who were among the first American Indians to live in the area, named the Platte River *Nebrathka*, which means "flat water."

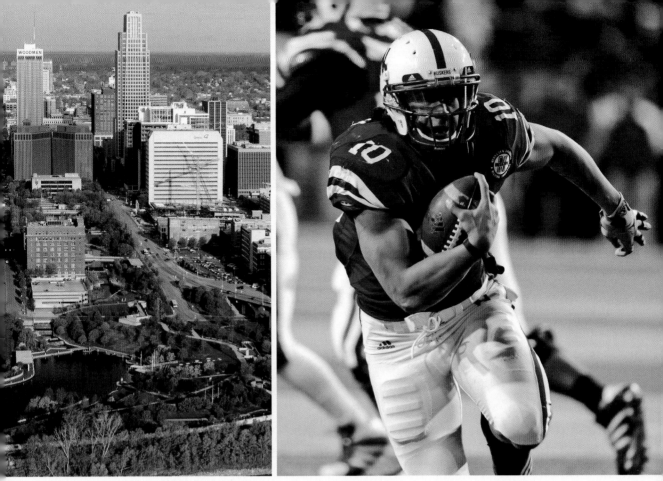

Omaha is the largest city in Nebraska and the 40th largest city in the United States.

Many Nebraskans are proud of the Cornhuskers, the football team representing the University of Nebraska The Cornhuskers have won several national championships over the years.

Nebraska is nicknamed the Cornhusker State after its main agricultural crop. Corn harvesting and the removal of husks were once done by hand. Large cornfields, wheat fields, and vast grazing lands have earned Nebraska the reputation as one of the world's best agricultural regions.

Nebraska's central location makes it easy to reach by roadways. It is within a one-day drive of many major cities, including Chicago, St. Louis, Kansas City, Minneapolis, Denver, and Salt Lake City. Interstate 80, an east–west route running across Nebraska, is one of the state's busiest highways. Several railroads carry freight through the state, and passenger trains serve the larger cities. Nebraska's busiest public airports are in Omaha, Lincoln, and Grand Island.

Where Is Nebraska?

I n the mid-1800s, thousands of pioneers crossed through Nebraska. The Platte River Valley became a westward route as people from the east headed for the rich farmland of Oregon and the gold mines of California. The Oregon, California, and Mormon trails were all very important routes that followed the Platte River as well as other river valleys.

At this time, Nebraska was regarded as little more than an access route to the west. Pioneers traveled through the region, mistakenly assuming that the dry land would be difficult to farm. The region was flat, sandy, and treeless. These features prompted the Nebraska region to be labeled the Great American Desert. As time passed, settlers decided to take on Nebraska's "desert," and they began to discover the rich resources the land had to offer.

Today people can hike, drive, or take a covered wagon tour of parts of the Oregon Trail. At Scotts Bluff National Monument, visitors can see an old covered wagon. They can learn about the journey by wagon across Nebraska more than 150 years ago.

Today most of the land in Nebraska is used for farming and grazing. Thanks to large irrigation systems, land that was once believed too dry for agriculture now yields an abundance of crops. Good soil for farmland has become one of Nebraska's most valuable resources. Also, the state's Sand Hills and grasslands are now vast grazing ranges that support large herds of cattle. Nebraska's agricultural abundance is not just a source of food. It is also a source of pride for many of the state's residents.

Nebraska is a state of surprising variety. It consists of widespread prairies, hundreds of small lakes, miles of sparkling rivers, dense hand-planted forests, and fascinating rock formations. Nebraskans are closely connected to their environment. The lakes, rivers, sands, prairies, and rolling hills have become part of Nebraska's charming identity and contribute to its people's livelihood.

I DIDN'T KNOW THAT!

The cottonwood became Nebraska's state tree in 1972. It was chosen to replace the elm, which had been the state tree since 1937, because most of the state's elm trees had been lost to disease.

The state insect of Nebraska is the honeybee.

Nebraska's state rock is prairie agate.

There are approximately 49,000 farms in Nebraska.

Many Nebraska farms use combines to harvest the wheat crop. As the combine moves across a field, it cuts the wheat, separates the seed from the stem, and cleans the wheat.

Mapping
Nebraska

Nebraska is bordered by six other states. South Dakota is to the north of Nebraska, while Iowa and Missouri are to the east. Kansas lies to the south. Colorado is to the west and south, and Wyoming is to the west. The Missouri River forms Nebraska's entire eastern border and part of its northern border.

Sites and Symbols

STATE SEAL
Nebraska

STATE BIRD
Western Meadowlark

STATE FLOWER
Goldenrod

STATE FLAG
Nebraska

STATE ANIMAL
White-Tailed Deer

STATE TREE
Cottonwood

Nickname The Cornhusker State

Motto Equality Before the Law

Song "Beautiful Nebraska," words by Jim Fras and Guy G. Miller, music by Jim Fras

Entered the Union March 1, 1867, as the 37th state

Capital Lincoln

Population (2010 Census) 1,826,341 Ranked 38th state

SOUTH DAKOTA

Mission •   Armour   Freeman   Canton   Rock Rapids   Spirit Lake

Spencer   Sioux Center

Le Mars   Storm Lake

WYOMING

Chadron   Gordon   Cody   Valentine   Spencer   Yankton   Vermillion

Ainsworth   Stuart   O Neill   Wayne   Sioux City   Sergeant Bluff

IOWA

NEBRASKA

Alliance   Thedford   Neligh   Norfolk   Onawa   Denison

Scottsbluff   Taylor   Bartlett   West Point   Dunlap

Broadwater   Ord   Columbus   Fremont   Blair   Missouri Valley

Oshkosh   Stapleton   Broken Bow   Ansley   David City   Wahoo   Omaha   Council Bluffs

Kimball   Sidney   Ogallala   North Platte   St. Paul   Central City   Papillion   Bellevue

Gothenburg   Grand Island   Seward   Ashland   Plattsmouth

Lexington   Kearney   Aurora   York   Milford   Lincoln   Clarinda

Maywood   Holdrege   Hastings   Geneva   Crete   Nebraska City

Minden   Beatrice   Auburn   **MO***

McCook   Hebron   Fairbury   Falls City

Stamford   Red Cloud   Superior   Hamburg

Brush   Wray

COLORADO

St. Francis   Oberlin   Norton   Smith Center   Mankato   Belleville   Marysville   Seneca   Hiawatha

KANSAS

Phillipsburg   Concordia   Horton

Crook   Sterling   Holyoke

*Missouri

N   Map Scale

0   100 Miles

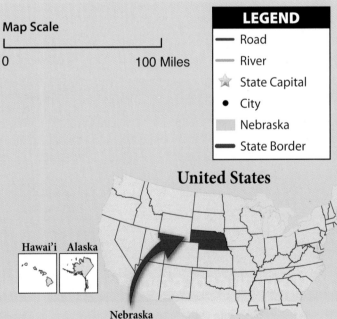

LEGEND

- ▬ Road
- ▬ River
- ★ State Capital
- ● City
- ▮ Nebraska
- ▬ State Border

United States

Hawai'i   Alaska

Nebraska

STATE CAPITAL

With a population of more than 250,000, Lincoln is the second-largest city in the state. It was founded in 1854 and chosen as the state capital in 1867. Lincoln is a regional center of government, finance, commerce, arts, education, and health care.

The Land

Nebraska's landscape consists of fertile, rolling plains. These plains are divided into two major land areas. The Dissected Till Plains cover the eastern fifth of the state. Several thousand years ago, glaciers covered the area. As the glaciers melted, they left behind debris, which served as the basis for extremely fertile soil. Today the area is made up of lowlands dissected, or divided up, by rivers and streams.

Most of Nebraska's landscape is dominated by the Great Plains, a land area that is largely grassland. The Sand Hills of the north-central part of the state are an interesting feature of the Great Plains. These vast hills were formed by the wind blowing sand that was originally deposited by glaciers. Today grasses help keep the sand in place.

TOADSTOOL GEOLOGIC PARK

Toadstool Geologic Park is located in the Oglala National Grassland in western Nebraska. It gets its name from the unusual rock formations in the park that look like toadstools. Fossils of prehistoric animals have been found in the park.

PLATTE RIVER

The Platte River flows southeast across Nebraska before emptying into the Missouri River. Pioneers followed the river west on the Oregon, California, and Mormon trails. More than a dozen dams on the river have decreased its width.

GREAT PLAINS

The Great Plains run north-south through the continental United States. They stretch from Montana to Texas, including much of Nebraska. They are a vast, high region of semiarid grassland.

SAND HILLS

The sloping hills and valleys of Nebraska's Sand Hills cover about one-fourth of the state. They are located in the north-central and northwestern part of Nebraska.

The highest point in Nebraska can be found in southwestern Kimball County. It is 5,426 feet above sea level.

A region that consists of **badlands** lies in the northwestern part of the state. This area has deep canyons, sandstone hills, and many deeply eroded rock formations.

The largest lake in Nebraska is Lake McConaughy. The lake was formed by damming part of the North Platte River. It has a surface area of 35,700 acres.

The Pine Ridge area in northwestern Nebraska contains 6,600 acres of trees, hills, and rolling plains.

The Loess Hills in eastern Nebraska are composed of windblown silt from the last Ice Age.

Nebraska winters can be very cold and snowy. Annual winter snowfalls vary between 21 inches in the southeast and about 45 inches in the northwest part of the state.

Climate

N ebraska experiences great seasonal changes in its weather. Winters can be bitterly cold, and summers can be uncomfortably hot. The weather can also change quickly. Warm air from the Gulf of Mexico occasionally collides with cool air from the north, which can result in severe weather. Tornadoes, blizzards, and violent thunderstorms are all common in the state.

The lowest recorded temperature in Nebraska was –47° Fahrenheit at Oshkosh on December 22, 1989. The highest recorded temperature was 118° F at Minden on July 24, 1936.

Average Annual Precipitation Across Nebraska

There can be great variation in precipitation among different cities in Nebraska. Why might Mitchell get less than half the rainfall that Omaha does?

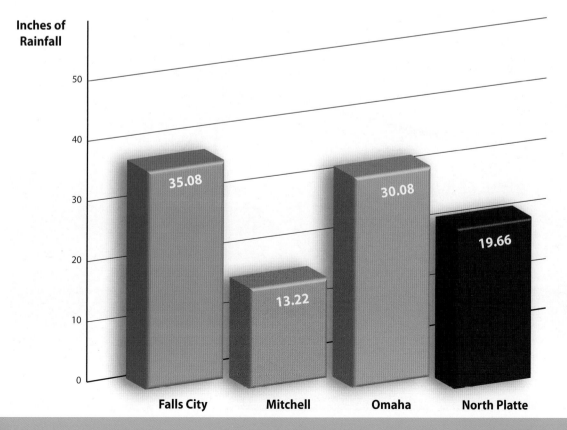

Inches of Rainfall

Falls City	35.08
Mitchell	13.22
Omaha	30.08
North Platte	19.66

Natural Resources

Water is one of Nebraska's greatest natural resources. The state has more than 2,000 small lakes and about 24,000 miles of rivers and streams. It also has one of the largest supplies of underground water in the nation. The Ogallala aquifer is a reserve of water located deep below most of Nebraska. Parts of this aquifer extend through Kansas, northwestern Oklahoma, and northwestern Texas. Water from the aquifer is pumped to the surface, and some of it is used to irrigate agricultural land in the region. Water is also stored in some of Nebraska's soil. In the Sand Hills the soil acts like a sponge, absorbing and holding the area's rainfall. The Platte River is also an important source of water.

Nebraska depends upon irrigation for a large part of its crop production. A great portion of the state's irrigated land is in the Platte River Valley.

Water and good soil make Nebraska ideal for farming. Nebraska's rich soil comes from deep deposits of **loess** in the eastern, central, and south-central parts of the state. Loess helps form some of the best agricultural soils in the country. More than 95 percent of Nebraska's land is used for agricultural purposes such as farming and ranching.

Among Nebraska's important minerals are limestone, sand, and gravel. Petroleum is found in the counties of Cheyenne, Hitchcock, Kimball, and Red Willow.

Half of Nebraska's cattle grazing takes place in the Sand Hills, an area with many streams and a variety of grasses. Grasses are a source of food for cattle.

Plants

Because only 2 percent of its land is forested, Nebraska is not well known for its trees. It is, however, known for its tree planting. In 1872, Nebraska became the first state to celebrate Arbor Day. A leader named J. Sterling Morton convinced the state board of agriculture to set aside a day to plant trees on the state's almost treeless landscape. Morton knew that the roots of the trees would draw much-needed moisture to the soil and help prevent erosion. In 1885, Arbor Day became a legal holiday in Nebraska, and today it is celebrated in many states throughout the country.

A large portion of Nebraska's hand-planted trees can be found in the Nebraska National Forest. The forest was established in 1902 as an experiment to see if trees could grow in the Sand Hills region. Today the Bessey Range district of the forest spans 90,000 acres. With about 22,000 acres of the forest planted by hand, it is the largest human-made forest in the United States.

BLUESTEM GRASS

Bluestem grass is native to Nebraska's prairies. There are several varieties, including little bluestem and big bluestem. It is often used as an ornamental grass in landscaping.

COTTONWOOD TREES

Cottonwood trees can be either male or female. The female trees produce fluffy white seeds that give the tree its name. Cottonwood trees often grow beside rivers.

GOLDENROD

Goldenrod has bright yellow flowers and can grow up to 4 feet high. It blooms in late summer and early autumn. Some people use the leaves for teas and medicinal purposes.

WILD BERGAMOT

Wild bergamot is a member of the mint family. Its flowers are red, pink, white, or lavender. Plants can grow as high as 5 feet. The leaves can be used to flavor tea.

I DIDN'T KNOW THAT!

Before it was nicknamed the Cornhusker State, Nebraska was known as the Tree Planter's State.

The prickly pear cactus is native to Nebraska's prairies. Its flat, fleshy pads are actually branches or stems.

Among Nebraska's few types of trees are pines and cedars, which are commonly found in the western regions. Ashes, cottonwoods, box elders, elms, oaks, walnuts, and willows can all be found in the central and eastern regions of the state.

Dozens of varieties of grasses are native to Nebraska's prairies.

During the spring, evening primroses bloom in Nebraska's eastern regions. In the summer, poppies, blue flags, larkspurs, and wild roses blossom in many parts of the state.

Animals

Millions of years ago, prehistoric animals roamed the Nebraska area. Scientists have uncovered fossil remains in Sioux County in the northwest corner of the state. Fossils of mammoths and **mastodons** have been found there. Other fossils from Sioux County suggest that Nebraska was once a tropical land. **Paleontologists** have uncovered remains of saber-toothed tigers, crocodiles, and rhinoceroses.

In more recent times, huge herds of bison, or buffalo, roamed Nebraska. But bison were killed in such large numbers when settlers came to the region that they almost disappeared from the area. Today Nebraska's wildlife consists mostly of small animals such as the badger, coyote, fox, muskrat, jackrabbit, raccoon, skunk, and squirrel. Mule deer also roam much of the region, and antelope and elk are found in the northwest. Game birds such as pheasants, quail, prairie chickens, and wild turkeys are all plentiful on Nebraska's prairies. The state's waters are full of bass, carp, trout, pike, crappies, and perch.

PRAIRIE CHICKEN

The prairie chicken is a game bird of the grouse family. Adults grow up to 18 inches long. During courtship, the male inflates air sacs in its throat. It makes booming noises from these inflated air sacs.

PRAIRIE RATTLESNAKE

The prairie rattlesnake lives in the grasses of western Nebraska's Great Plains. In the winter, the snakes live together in sites that do not freeze, such as the burrows of other animals. They feed on small mammals.

PRAIRIE DOG

The black-tailed prairie dog is the only prairie dog species found in Nebraska, in the western two-thirds of the state. Prairie dogs are highly social animals. Their colonies can be recognized by the holes and mounds at the entrance. A colony has as many as 50 burrow entrances per acre.

PRONGHORN

Pronghorns can be found only on North America's Great Plains. The male's horns average about 12 inches and are shed yearly. The female sometimes develops smaller horns. With a top speed of 60 miles per hour, a pronghorn can outrun any animal that chases it.

Tourism

Nebraska has many natural, historical, and cultural attractions. Tourists may retrace the water route of the Lewis and Clark Expedition, view fossil excavation sites, or visit the Strategic Air and Space Museum near the Eugene T. Mahoney State Park.

Nebraska is a great place for history buffs. Several forts and pioneer museums offer a glimpse of what life was like for Nebraska's early settlers. The Stuhr Museum of the Prairie Pioneer allows visitors to relive Nebraska's past with Old West **memorabilia** and American Indian artifacts. There is also a railroad town in the museum that takes visitors back to a time when western towns had wooden sidewalks and posts for tying horses. This town boasts 60 original buildings from the late 1800s.

SCOTTS BLUFF NATIONAL MONUMENT

Scotts Bluff towers 800 feet above the North Platte River. It was a landmark for thousands of settlers who crossed the Great Plains in covered wagons in the 1800s. At Scotts Bluff National Monument, summertime visitors can relive life on the Oregon Trail through a Living History program.

CHIMNEY ROCK NATIONAL HISTORIC SITE

Chimney Rock is one of the most famous landmarks on the Oregon, California, and Mormon trails. The rock formation rises nearly 300 feet above the surrounding North Platte River valley. Its peak is 4,226 feet above sea level. It is estimated that nearly half a million settlers saw Chimney Rock as they made their way westward.

HENRY DOORLY ZOO

Omaha's Henry Doorly Zoo is ranked one of the best zoos in the nation. It has a huge aquarium and the world's largest enclosed rain forest. Hubbard Gorilla Valley is a $14 million, three-acre exhibit at the zoo.

CARHENGE

Carhenge, near Alliance, is a re-creation of ancient Stonehenge in Wiltshire, England, but in place of giant stones, the builders of Carhenge used old cars. In 2009 Carhenge was named the second wackiest attraction in the United States.

Fort Robinson State Park and Museum was a military post from 1874 to 1948. Today visitors can sleep in the original and rebuilt buildings of the fort.

Buffalo Bill Cody built his Scout's Rest Ranch in North Platte in 1886. This was during the heyday of his world-renowned Wild West Show. Today the ranch has been restored and is a Nebraska state park.

Some Nebraska highways follow the historic Oregon and Mormon trails that once led pioneers to the West.

At the Lincoln Children's Zoo visitors can watch butterflies emerge from their cocoon state.

Industry

griculture is a vital part of Nebraska's economy. Nebraska ranks third, behind Texas and Kansas, for its number of beef cattle. Hog production is also important to Nebraska's economy. The Cornhusker State is a leading corn producer. Its annual corn crop is the third-largest of any state in the country. Other important crops in Nebraska include soybeans, hay, sorghum, and wheat.

Industries in Nebraska
Value of Goods and Services in Millions of Dollars

Although Nebraska is known as an agricultural state, many different industries are important. Which other industries could be thought of as offshoots of the part of the economy that is directly agricultural?

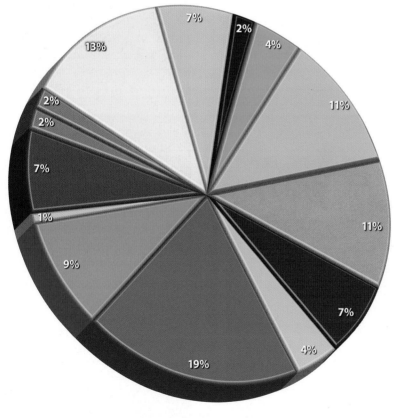

LEGEND

	Agriculture, Forestry, and Fishing	$5,957
*	Mining	$108
	Utilities	$1,624
	Construction	$3,372
	Manufacturing	$9,653
	Wholesale and Retail Trade	$9,873
	Transportation	$6,397
	Media and Entertainment	$3,058
	Finance, Insurance, and Real Estate	$16,469
	Professional and Technical Services	$7,767
	Education	$723
	Health Care	$6,125
	Hotels and Restaurants	$1,819
	Other Services	$2,095
	Government	$11,058

TOTAL $86,099

*Less than 1%. Percentages may not add to 100 because of rounding.

Corn is the leading crop in Nebraska, in terms of acres planted and farm receipts. More than 30 percent of Nebraska's farm receipts come from corn.

Nebraska's agricultural goods are central to food processing, one of the state's other major industries. The food manufacturing industry uses the state's agricultural products as its **raw materials**. Nebraska is one of the nation's chief producers of meat and grain products. Large meatpacking plants can be found in Dakota City, Fremont, Grand Island, Lexington, Omaha, and Gibbon. Breakfast cereal, livestock feed, and bread are all important grain-based products processed in the state.

Manufacturing food products accounts for about one-third of all manufacturing in Nebraska.

Goods and Services

Nebraska's central location is responsible for its thriving transportation industry. For hundreds of years people have used the Platte River Valley as a transportation route. In 1865 Omaha became the eastern **terminus** of the first transcontinental railroad in the United States. Railroad companies then began laying track westward, making Omaha an important center for railroad transport. Today the Union Pacific Railroad has its headquarters in Omaha, and other major rail lines also provide freight service to the state.

Omaha is not only one of the nation's chief rail centers, it is also a major financial center. Many of the country's largest insurance companies and **telemarketing** businesses have their head offices there. Lincoln is also an important insurance center and a leading **wholesale** and retail trade center.

Coal makes up much of the freight transported through Nebraska. The state has the largest freight rail yard in the world.

State aid to education has increased greatly in the past 50 years. At the same time, the number of school districts has been reduced, so that money and facilities can be used more efficiently.

Many Nebraskans have jobs with the federal or state government. Government services in the state include the operation of electrical utilities, public hospitals, and military bases. The headquarters of the United States Strategic Command, or USSTRATCOM, are on Offutt Air Force Base near Omaha. The Command Center controls the country's bombers and long-range missiles.

With a large number of teachers working in the state's schools, the public school system is a major employer in Nebraska. Students are given many opportunities for higher learning in the state. The University of Nebraska, which opened in 1869, has campuses in Omaha, Lincoln, and Kearney. Other major universities and colleges throughout the state offer programs of study in a variety of fields. Among these schools are Peru State College, Nebraska Wesleyan University, Bellevue University, and Creighton University.

American Indians

Centuries before European explorers made their way to Nebraska, many groups of American Indians lived in the area. Among those who farmed and hunted along the rivers were the Mission, Omaha, Oto, and Ponca. The Pawnee were the largest group to settle along Nebraska's Platte, Republican, and Loup rivers. They hunted bison and grew crops such as corn and beans. The Pawnee were also known to fight against other tribes who lived in the western part of what is now Nebraska.

The Pawnee believed that some of the stars were gods, and they used their knowledge of the stars to regulate activities such as planting corn. They also thought of corn as a symbolic mother through whom the sun god gave blessings to the people.

The Pawnees lived in earthen lodges that were supported by posts. The lodges were recessed about 3 feet into the ground. About 300 to 500 Pawnees lived together in villages.

The groups in western Nebraska relied mostly on hunting for their livelihood. These groups included the Sioux, Comanche, Cheyenne, and Arapaho. They were all **nomadic** peoples. They lived in temporary villages, following and hunting bison and other game. Because their livelihood depended on hunting, these groups worked together to defend their hunting grounds against the Pawnee and early white settlers.

Religion was a major focus in the life of the Sioux people. The most important religious occasion was the yearly Sun Dance. At this ceremony, groups of Sioux gathered to perform acts of individual and community sacrifice, which they believed would maintain their connection to the universe as a whole.

The Sioux were a confederation of American Indian tribes. They lived on the Plains and spoke similar languages. Sioux women carried their babies on their backs.

Explorers

I n 1541 the Spanish explorer Francisco Vázquez de Coronado led
an expedition across the southwestern United States. Coronado
claimed a large area for Spain that included present-day Nebraska.
In 1682, René-Robert Cavelier, sieur de La Salle, traveled down the
Mississippi River. He claimed all the land drained by the Mississippi
River for France. La Salle named this vast area Louisiana after his king,
Louis XIV. By the end of the 1600s both Spain and France had claimed
the Nebraska region without ever having set foot in the area.

The first recorded European to enter Nebraska was a French explorer
named Etienne Veniard de Bourgmont. In 1714 he traveled up the
Missouri River to the mouth
of the Platte and built a
trading post. Other French
pioneers followed, but more
local exploration was to come.
In the early 1800s, what is now
Nebraska was part of France's
Louisiana Territory. In 1803
the United States bought
this vast tract of land in the
western Mississippi River
basin. Costing less than three
cents per acre, the Louisiana
Purchase is considered one
of the greatest land bargains
in U.S. history. Soon after,
President Thomas Jefferson
sent Meriwether Lewis and
William Clark to explore
the territory.

When René-Robert Cavelier, sieur de La Salle, claimed the
Mississippi River Basin for France in 1682, that claim included
the land of present-day Nebraska. Nebraska's rivers drain into
the Missouri River, which drains into the Mississippi.

Timeline of Settlement

Early Exploration

1682 René-Robert Cavelier, sieur de La Salle, claims Nebraska for France.

1714 Etienne Veniard de Bourgmont establishes a trading post on the Platte River.

U.S. Exploration

1803 The United States purchases the Louisiana Territory, including Nebraska, from France.

1804 Lewis and Clark's expedition to explore the Louisiana Territory passes through Nebraska.

1806 Zebulon Pike explores southern Nebraska.

1810 A fur trading post is established at Bellevue.

U.S. Territory and Statehood

1820 Fort Atkinson is established by the U.S. Army.

1843 Pioneers begin traveling in large numbers through Nebraska on the Oregon Trail.

1848 Fort Kearny is built to protect settlers on the Oregon Trail.

1854 Nebraska is made a separate territory by the Kansas-Nebraska Act.

1861 The **Pony Express** passes through Nebraska, carrying mail from Missouri to California.

1867 Nebraska becomes the 37th state.

Early Settlers

Explorers and fur traders from the eastern United States soon
followed Lewis and Clark to the Nebraska wilderness. In the
early 1800s several trading posts were built along the Missouri
River. To protect its newly claimed territory, the U.S. government built
Fort Atkinson in 1820. It was home to as many as 1,000 people, mostly
soldiers and their families, until it was abandoned seven years later.

Map of Settlements and Resources in Early Nebraska

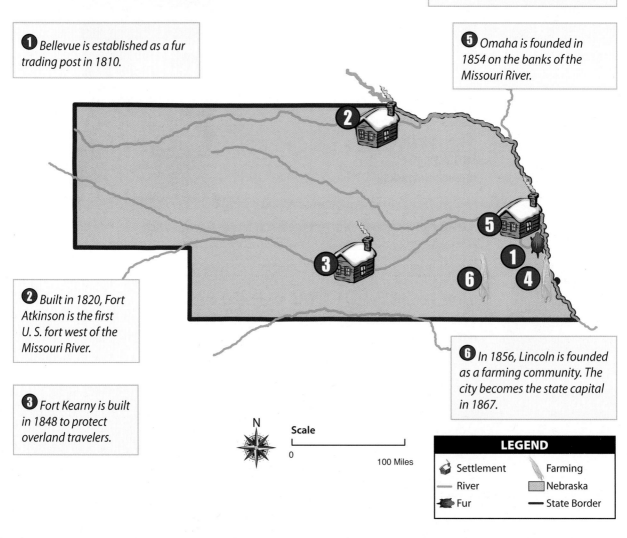

❹ Plattsmouth is founded in 1854 as a farming community where the Platte and Missouri rivers meet.

❶ Bellevue is established as a fur trading post in 1810.

❺ Omaha is founded in 1854 on the banks of the Missouri River.

❷ Built in 1820, Fort Atkinson is the first U. S. fort west of the Missouri River.

❸ Fort Kearny is built in 1848 to protect overland travelers.

❻ In 1856, Lincoln is founded as a farming community. The city becomes the state capital in 1867.

N

Scale

0   100 Miles

LEGEND	
🪵 Settlement	Farming
— River	Nebraska
Fur	State Border

In 1854 the U.S. government passed the Kansas-Nebraska Act. This act created the Kansas and Nebraska territories and opened the region for settlement. Settlers from the eastern states began to arrive. Nebraska's first towns sprang up along or near the Missouri River. By 1860 more than 28,000 people lived in the region.

The Homestead Act of 1862 brought a rush of eager pioneers to the Nebraska Territory. The act granted 160 free acres of western **frontier** land to any settler who farmed it. Settlers would own the land after they had farmed it for five years. This offer encouraged thousands of homesteaders to make their way to Nebraska. During the late 1800s the new farmers had plenty of bad luck. They suffered through some very cold winters and long periods of drought. There was also a brief period when swarms of grasshoppers plagued the area, ruining crops. Discouraged, many farmers left the plains. Still, others remained, and before long, improved farming techniques brought more settlers to Nebraska.

With few trees in the Nebraska region, early settlers had to build their homes with **sod**. These settlers were nicknamed Sodbusters.

Notable People

Many notable Nebraskans have contributed to the development of their state and their country. One even became the president of the United States. Other people helped minority groups struggle for their rights. Some Nebraskans wrote books and produced films about the American experience. Businessmen and religious leaders have helped other people achieve success and made Nebraskans proud.

**WILLA CATHER
(1873–1947)**

Willa Cather was an American novelist noted for her portrayal of pioneer life on the American plains. She grew up in Red Cloud and used her memories as material for her writing. Her most well-known books about Nebraska are *O Pioneers!* and *My Ántonia*.

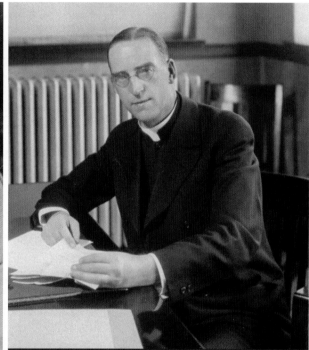

**FATHER EDWARD FLANAGAN
(1886–1948)**

Father Edward Joseph Flanagan founded Father Flanagan's Home for Boys in Omaha in 1917. This was a home and school intended to provide support and education for neglected or troubled boys. The home was moved west of Omaha in 1918 and quickly became incorporated as Boys Town. Eighty-one similar programs around the world now operate based on Father Flanagan's example.

GERALD R. FORD (1913–2006)

Gerald Ford was born in Omaha but moved to Michigan as a child. He served in Congress as a representative from Michigan for 25 years. Then he served as vice president. In 1974 he became the United States' 39th president when Richard Nixon resigned.

MALCOM X (1925–1965)

Born Malcolm Little in Omaha, Malcolm X became a vocal leader in the early 1960s. He joined the Nation of Islam, also known as the Black Muslims, and helped increase the group's membership. He urged African Americans to take pride in their race. His writings, including *The Autobiography of Malcolm X*, continue to inspire many people.

WARREN BUFFETT (1930–)

Warren Buffett grew up in Omaha. His father was a stockbroker and served as a U.S. congressman. At an early age Buffett showed a knack for financial matters. He took control of the manufacturing company Berkshire Hathaway in 1965. His shrewd investing led him to become one of the world's wealthiest men. In 2006, Buffett announced that he was giving away more than 80 percent of his wealth to private charity foundations.

Red Cloud (1822–1909) was a chief of the Oglala Teton Sioux. He resisted the U.S. government takeover of Indian lands and acted as a spokesman for his people's rights. Between 1865 and 1867 he and his followers kept the government from building the Bozeman Trail to goldfields in the Montana Territory.

Darryl F. Zanuck (1902–1979) was born in Wahoo and moved to Los Angeles in the early 1920s. He co-founded Twentieth Century Pictures in 1933. Zanuck is known for producing many successful films, including *The Grapes of Wrath, The Longest Day*, and *The Sound of Music*.

 Population

According to the 2010 U.S. Census, Nebraska had a population of 1,826,341 as of April 1 of that year. Its population had grown by almost 7 percent in the decade from 2000 to 2010. In the early 1900s more than two thirds of Nebraskans lived in rural areas. As time passed, this number shifted dramatically. Many people left rural areas because of the growing employment opportunities in the state's towns and cities. Today most Nebraskans live in urban areas. The population is especially dense around the state's two largest cities, Omaha and Lincoln. More than half of all Nebraskans live in these two **metropolitan** areas.

Nebraska's urban areas are almost all located in the eastern part of the state. However, a few densely populated areas can be found along the Platte and North Platte rivers.

Nebraska Population 1950–2010

Nebraska's population has grown slowly but steadily since the middle of the 20th century. What are some possible reasons why the population has not grown more quickly?

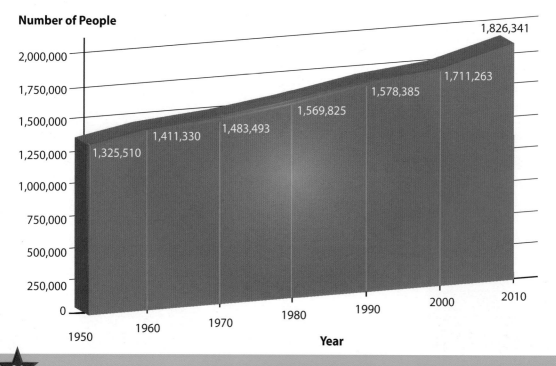

Some north and central areas of Nebraska are sparsely populated. In fact, some counties have an average of fewer than five residents per square mile.

Omaha and Lincoln are less than 60 miles apart.

About a dozen counties in Nebraska have fewer than 1,000 people each.

Omaha has about 455,000 people within its city limits. Lincoln is home to about 254,000 people.

After Omaha and Lincoln, Nebraska's largest cities are Bellevue, Grand Island, Kearney, Hastings, and Fremont.

Omaha is the commercial, manufacturing, and telecommunications center of Nebraska. More than 1.2 million people live within 50 miles of Omaha, making up the Greater Omaha area.

Politics and Government

Nebraska's government is unique among all the states in the nation. Like other states, Nebraska has an executive branch of government that is headed by a governor. Like most other states, Nebraska has a judicial system that is headed by a Supreme Court. But Nebraska is the only state in the Union to have a **unicameral** legislature. Every other state legislature has two houses, or chambers, not one.

Construction of Nebraska's Capitol began in 1922. It took 10 years to complete and cost about $10 million. Its tower is 400 feet high and is visible for miles around.

Nebraska's legislature was not always unicameral. In 1934, Nebraskans voted to rid themselves of half their state legislature. People felt that a unicameral formation would be more democratic and would allow more public awareness of the legislature's actions. In 1937 the first session of the state's unicameral legislature was held. Today there are 49 members in the legislature. These members are referred to as senators, and each of them serves a term of four years.

In the U.S. Congress, Nebraska, like all other states, has two senators in the U.S. Senate. Nebraska has three members in the U.S. House of Representatives, where the number of seats each state has depends on its population. Because Nebraska's population is relatively small, about two-thirds of the states have more House members than Nebraska does.

The Memorial Chamber of the Capitol building is dedicated to heroism in public service. The use of black marble adds to the chamber's dignity. The dome represents the evening sky and the chandelier, the stars shining in it.

I DIDN'T KNOW THAT!

Nebraska's state song is called "Beautiful Nebraska."

Here are the words of the song:

Beautiful Nebraska,
    peaceful prairieland,
Laced with many rivers,
    and the hills of sand;
Dark green valleys cradled
    in the earth,
Rain and sunshine bring
    abundant birth.

Beautiful Nebraska, as you
    look around,
You will find a rainbow
    reaching to the ground;
All these wonders by the
    Master's hand;
Beautiful Nebraska land.

We are so proud of this state
    where we live,
There is no place that has
    so much to give.

Cultural Groups

During the 1800s thousands of Europeans came to Nebraska in search of free or inexpensive land to farm. German, Swedish, Czech, and Irish **immigrants** flocked to the region. Many people who live in Nebraska today are their descendants. Many of them work hard to preserve the cultural traditions of their ancestors.

A large number of the state's ethnic communities are concentrated in specific villages or towns. The village of Wausa, for example, has many people of Swedish descent. The Wausa Community Swedish Smorgasbord is held every October. For more than 50 years the event has celebrated Swedish traditions with colorful costumes, food, and music. In Wilber the annual National Czech Festival showcases Czech culture with arts, crafts, and food.

Every August between 30,000 and 50,000 people flock to the Czech Festival in the tiny town of Wilber. Local residents dress in authentic folk costumes, and visitors can watch dancers perform folk dances. Traditional Czech dishes such as potato dumplings and spicy sausages are served as well.

Nebraska's American Indians actively preserve and share their cultural traditions through colorful and lively **powwow** celebrations. During the first full moon in August, the Omaha Tribe of Nebraska hosts a powwow to celebrate the harvest. This powwow is the oldest harvest celebration in the state.

There are many events and sites throughout Nebraska that pay tribute to the state's frontier and pioneer heritage. Cowboy museums in Gordon and Ogallala recognize the ranching traditions and activities that continue to be a large part of Nebraska life. Pioneer museums, festivals, and landmarks showcase Nebraska's important historic figures and events. Every year in Lincoln, Nebraskans celebrate their state during the Nebraska State Fair, which features Nebraskan talent, including local arts and crafts.

The Hispanic population of Nebraska has been growing in recent years. The state is home to about 150,000 Hispanic Americans, more than twice the number who lived in Nebraska in the year 2000. Hispanic Americans represent more than 8 percent of the state's population. Most of them are people of Mexican heritage.

Powwows feature traditional music, dancing, foods, and beadwork. The Native American Association at Creighton University in Omaha holds an All-Nations Powwow every year in April.

Arts and Entertainment

Many popular entertainers are from the state of Nebraska. Actors such as Nick Nolte, Marlon Brando, and Henry Fonda were born in the Cornhusker State. Other well-known Cornhuskers include Fred Astaire, a dancer and film actor, and comedian Johnny Carson.

Nebraska's entertainment scene is not limited to the Cornhuskers who left for Hollywood and Broadway. The state supports many impressive theatrical troupes and programs for theater, music, and dance lovers. Omaha is a major center for the arts in Nebraska. Among the city's theaters are the Omaha Theater Company for Young People and the Omaha Magic Theater. The Omaha Community Playhouse is among the largest community theaters in the United States and

boasts a professional touring company called the Nebraska Theater Caravan. The Orpheum Theater/ Omaha Performing Arts Center houses the Omaha Symphony and the Omaha Theater Ballet. The Orpheum also houses Opera Omaha, one of the nation's most progressive opera companies.

The Omaha Symphony presents more than 200 live performances throughout the year, in Omaha and across Nebraska and Iowa. Some of the symphony's concerts are directed toward children and youth.

The performing arts thrive in other parts of the state, too. The Lincoln Community Playhouse puts on engaging performances, and the Lincoln Symphony Orchestra entertains listeners with musical works. The Lied Center for Performing Arts, at the University of Nebraska at Lincoln, presents nationally and internationally recognized performers and speakers. Many of Nebraska's smaller cities and towns have strong music and theater programs at their universities and colleges.

Nebraska is as rich in visual arts as it is in performing arts. Omaha's Joslyn Art Museum has one of the finest art collections of the American West in the country. It also has exhibits of classic and modern works, all of which are housed in a beautiful marble building. The Sheldon Memorial Art Gallery and Sculpture Garden is on the grounds of the University of Nebraska at Lincoln. It has fascinating displays of 20th-century North American paintings and sculpture as well as 18th-century landscapes and still-life paintings. The Museum of Nebraska Art in Kearney has 11 galleries showcasing works of art by Nebraska artists.

Hilary Swank was born in 1974 in Lincoln. She and her mother moved to Los Angeles when Hilary was a child, and she began auditioning for parts in films and TV series. She got her break in 1992, when she appeared in Buffy the Vampire Slayer. *She has won two Academy Awards for Best Actress since then, for her work in* Boys Don't Cry *in 1999 and* Million Dollar Baby *in 2004.*

Sports

Nebraskans have no major professional sports teams to cheer on, but their commitment to college athletics is outstanding. The University of Nebraska recruits and trains some of the finest young athletes in the country. Cornhuskers teams compete against other colleges and universities in such sports as football, volleyball, basketball, and baseball.

The college football season draws Nebraska's most lively and enthusiastic fans. The Cornhuskers are traditionally a strong football team and have finished many seasons as one of the top teams in the country. They have also won numerous conference championships. When at home, the team plays at the University of Nebraska's Memorial Stadium in Lincoln, where loyal fans pack the stadium. Season tickets to Cornhuskers games are highly valued by Nebraska sports fans.

Born in Omaha in 1982, Andy Roddick is one of the top tennis players in the world. He won his first Grand Slam tournament title in 2003, the same year he was named Player of the Year by the Association of Tennis Professionals, or ATP.

Nebraska is known for its rodeos. The state's first rodeo was put on in the 1880s by William Cody, known as Buffalo Bill Cody. Buffalo Bill was one of the best-known cowboys of the Old West. He was a Pony Express rider, army scout, and buffalo hunter. In 1882, Buffalo Bill put together a special celebration for the Fourth of July at his ranch in North Platte. What he organized is thought to have been the first official rodeo in the nation. Today the Buffalo Bill Rodeo is held every June near the town of North Platte.

One of the state's most popular rodeos is called Nebraska's Big Rodeo and is held each July in Burwell. In fact, Burwell's rodeo grounds are active all summer long with ranch rodeos and professional rodeos. There are several other county and community rodeos held throughout the state.

Rodeo reflects the talents and skills of working cowboys. Different rodeo events test those skills. Popular events include calf roping, steer wrestling, bareback riding, and bull riding.

I DIDN'T KNOW THAT!

Lincoln is the site of the National Museum of Roller Skating. The museum has the world's largest collection of historical roller skates and roller-skating memorabilia. It also has displays on roller disco, trick skaters, and skating animals.

The forests and rugged rock formations in Nebraska's Pine Ridge area are popular destinations for hikers, cyclists, and campers.

Every spring Omaha hosts the National Collegiate Athletic Association's men's baseball world series games.

The Omaha Lancers compete in the United States Hockey League, a junior league.

Nebraskans inducted into the Baseball Hall of Fame include pitcher Bob Gibson, who won 251 games and struck out 3,117 batters in his career.

National Averages Comparison

The United States is a federal republic, consisting of fifty states and the District of Columbia. Alaska and Hawai'i are the only non-contiguous, or non-touching, states in the nation. Today, the United States of America is the third-largest country in the world in population. The United States Census Bureau takes a census, or count of all the people, every ten years. It also regularly collects other kinds of data about the population and the economy. How does Nebraska compare with the national average?

Comparison Chart

United States 2010 Census Data *	USA	Nebraska
Admission to Union	NA	March 1, 1867
Land Area (in square miles)	3,537,438.44	76,872.41
Population Total	308,745,538	1,826,341
Population Density (people per square mile)	87.28	23.76
Population Percentage Change (April 1, 2000, to April 1, 2010)	9.7%	6.7%
White Persons (percent)	72.4%	86.1%
Black Persons (percent)	12.6%	4.5%
American Indian and Alaska Native Persons (percent)	0.9%	1.0%
Asian Persons (percent)	4.8%	1.8%
Native Hawaiian and Other Pacific Islander Persons (percent)	0.2%	0.1%
Some Other Race (percent)	6.2%	4.3%
Persons Reporting Two or More Races (percent)	2.9%	2.2%
Persons of Hispanic or Latino Origin (percent)	16.3%	9.2%
Not of Hispanic or Latino Origin (percent)	83.7%	90.8%
Median Household Income	$52,029	$49,731
Percentage of People Age 25 or Over Who Have Graduated from High School	80.4%	86.6%

*All figures are based on the 2010 United States Census, with the exception of the last two items.

How to Improve My Community

Strong communities make strong states. Think about what features are important in your community. What do you value? Education? Health? Forests? Safety? Beautiful spaces? Government works to help citizens create ideal living conditions that are fair to all by providing services in communities. Consider what changes you could make in your community. How would they improve your state as a whole? Using this concept web as a guide, write a report that outlines the features you think are most important in your community and what improvements could be made. A strong state needs strong communities.

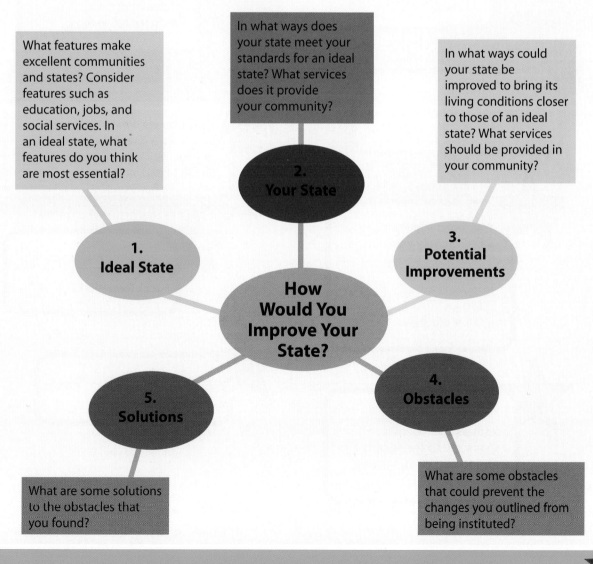

What features make excellent communities and states? Consider features such as education, jobs, and social services. In an ideal state, what features do you think are most essential?

In what ways does your state meet your standards for an ideal state? What services does it provide your community?

In what ways could your state be improved to bring its living conditions closer to those of an ideal state? What services should be provided in your community?

2. Your State

1. Ideal State

3. Potential Improvements

How Would You Improve Your State?

5. Solutions

4. Obstacles

What are some solutions to the obstacles that you found?

What are some obstacles that could prevent the changes you outlined from being instituted?

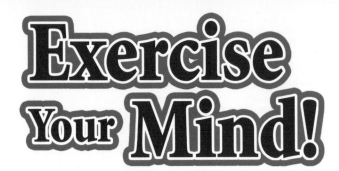

Exercise Your Mind!

Think about these questions and then use your research skills to find the answers and learn more fascinating facts about Nebraska. A teacher, librarian, or parent may be able to help you locate the best sources to use in your research.

1 True or False? One of the world's largest mammoth fossils was found in Nebraska.

2 True or False? Nebraska's Cherry County is larger than the state of Connecticut.

3 Which of the following is a town in Nebraska?

a) Friend
b) Beaver City
c) Wahoo
d) All of the above

4 One of Nebraska's biggest festivals and rodeos is sponsored by the Knights of Ak-Sar-Ben. What is special about that name?

5 What tasty beverage was invented in Nebraska?

a) Coca Cola®
b) Root beer
c) Kool-Aid®
d) Chocolate milk

6 Take a guess! What area in Nebraska is one of the most productive cattle-raising regions in the United States?

7 True or False? Toadstool Park is named for rock formations.

8 Where was the world's first test-tube tiger born?

Words to Know

badlands: a barren area with interesting rock formations

corridor: land that links two areas or that follows a road or river

frontier: land that forms the furthest boundary of inhabited regions

hydroelectric: water-generated electricity

immigrants: people who move to a new country

irrigation: supplying dry land with water through human-made processes

loess: a yellowish sandy soil that is carried by wind

mastodons: large, extinct, elephant-like mammals

memorabilia: souvenirs and historical items associated with particular times or subjects

metropolitan: large or busy, as in highly populated urban areas

nomadic: moving from place to place, often in search of food

paleontologists: scientists who study prehistoric remains, such as fossils

Pony Express: a system of mail delivery in the mid-1800s. Mail carriers rode ponies between Missouri and California.

powwow: an American Indian ceremony or festival

raw materials: materials that have not yet been processed but will be used in making a product

sod: a piece of earth, usually covered in grass or roots

telemarketing: selling or marketing things over the telephone

terminus: the end of a railroad route

unicameral: a legislature that consists of only one house

wholesale: related to the selling of goods in large quantities to someone who will resell them

Index

Log on to www.av2books.com

AV² by Weigl brings you media enhanced books that support active learning. Go to www.av2books.com, and enter the special code found on page 2 of this book. You will gain access to enriched and enhanced content that supplements and complements this book. Content includes video, audio, web links, quizzes, a slide show, and activities.

Audio
Listen to sections of the book read aloud.

Video
Watch informative video clips.

Embedded Weblinks
Gain additional information for research.

Try This!
Complete activities and hands-on experiments.

WHAT'S ONLINE?

Try This!	Embedded Weblinks	Video	EXTRA FEATURES
Test your knowledge of the state in a mapping activity.	Discover more attractions in Nebraska.	Watch a video introduction to Nebraska.	**Audio** Listen to sections of the book read aloud.
Find out more about precipitation in your city.	Learn more about the history of the state.	Watch a video about the features of the state.	
Plan what attractions you would like to visit in the state.	Learn the full lyrics of the state song.		**Key Words** Study vocabulary, and complete a matching word activity.
Learn more about the early natural resources of the state.			
Write a biography about a notable resident of Nebraska.			**Slide Show** View images and captions, and prepare a presentation
Complete an educational census activity.			**Quizzes** Test your knowledge.

AV² was built to bridge the gap between print and digital. We encourage you to tell us what you like and what you want to see in the future.

Sign up to be an AV² Ambassador at www.av2books.com/ambassador.

Due to the dynamic nature of the Internet, some of the URLs and activities provided as part of AV² by Weigl may have changed or ceased to exist. AV² by Weigl accepts no responsibility for any such changes. All media enhanced books are regularly monitored to update addresses and sites in a timely manner. Contact AV² by Weigl at 1-866-649-3445 or av2books@weigl.com with any questions, comments, or feedback.